200 A  DOG FACTS

FOR KIDS AND ADULTS:

Learn about the weirdest dog facts that will impress you and your friends

ANTHONY PORTOKALOGLOU

Copyright © 2017 by Anthony Portokaloglou

All rights reserved. No part of this publication may be reproduced, distributed or transmitted in any form or by any means, without prior written permission from the author.

Disclaimer Notice

The content in this book are for informational purposes only. All attempts have been made by the author to provide real and accurate content. No responsibility will be taken by the author for any damages cost by misuse of the content described in this book. Please consult a licensed professional before utilizing the information of this book.

Legal Disclaimer

The photos in this book are licensed for commercial use or in the public domain

Contents

INDRODUCTION..5

200 DOG FACTS..7

CONCLUSION 119

INDRODUCTION

You probably know some of the 200 dog facts in this book, but you will find it difficult to believe some of the weirdest dog facts found on this list.

Dogs...

These fascinating, intelligent, loving and loyal creatures are easy to overlook just how incredible they are.

But...

That is about to change as from today. Read out these 200 bizarre dog facts every dog lover must know.

200 DOG FACTS

1. As we have noticed dogs seem predisposed to chase their tails. They do this for several reasons. It might be due to being curious, they may need exercise, or even some form of predatory instinct. It could be anxiety or even fleas. Chasing their tail is normal dog behavior, but if he/she begins to do it excessively; you will want to talk with your vet.

----

2. Were you aware that puppies only have 28 teeth? The average adult dog boasts of 42 teeth.

---

3. We all enjoy the beautiful spots of a Dalmatian dog! Were you aware that when they are puppies they are

pure white? The spots develop later as they become older.

---

4. Have you ever watched your dog twitching and moving their paws during a nap? It has been discovered that dogs and humans both enjoy the same type of slow wave sleep (SWS) as well as the same rapid eye movement (REM).

It is fun to imagine what your pet could be dreaming about. Perhaps chasing a cat or a bunny?

---

5. Did you know that dogs are gifted with night vision? Their eyes contain a unique membrane known

as the tapetum. This membrane helps them to see in the dark.

---

6. Have you ever wondered about your dog's heart beat? If your dog is a large breed, then the resting heart rate is between 60 and 100 times each minute. If your dog is a small breed, then the resting heart rate is between 100 and 140 times each minute. We humans generally have a resting heart rate of 60 to 100 times each minute.

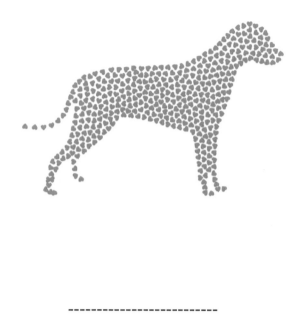

----

7. A dog's normal temperature would be considered high for a human. Human's average at 98.6 degrees, but a dog's normal temperature is between 101 and 102.5 degrees.

----

8. Dogs have a unique place in which they release sweat! They sweat through their foot pads. Humans in comparison can sweat all over their body!

----

9. We think of green aliens from Mars having unique eyelids, but did you know that a dog has three eyelids? The dog has both and upper and lower lid; but also a third lid. The

third lid is called a nictitating membrane or is sometimes referred to as the "haw". This enables the dog's eye to stay moist and protected.

----

10. The homes which have a pet equal to about 62% of United State's houses. This means that approximately 72.9 million homes have a pet!

----

11. When your dog licks his nose he is actually intensifying his ability to smell. There is a thin layer of mucous that helps a dog to absorb the smell. The dog will then lick his nose to get the scent in his mouth.

---

12. Have you ever wondered why a dog can eat some of the things that he/she does, like something really gross and actually enjoy it? Dogs only have around 1,700 taste buds

compared to a human's 9,000 taste buds. Cats average around 473.

----

13. Oftentimes a dog will get excited about a smell that you can't even begin to smell. The reason is that a dog has a sense of smell that is 10,000 – 100,000 times more sensitive that we humans.

---

14. Some people claim that dogs can only see in black and white. This has been discovered to be a myth. It is now believed that dogs mainly see in blues, greenish-yellows and also different shades of gray.

----

15. Hertz is the measure of sound. The higher Hertz will be higher in pitch. Dogs can hear easily at 8,000 Hz. Humans normal hearing range is about 2,000 Hz.

----

16. Dogs can get their ears into all sorts of different positions. The reason for this is because dogs have more than a dozen different muscles to

control their ears and how they move.

----

17. Have you ever noticed that a Chow Chow will have a blueish black tongue? Did you know their tongues are pink when they are born? Around 8 – 10 weeks of age their tongues will change colors.

---

18. Have you seen a dog kicking up in the grass after they have finished eliminating? They use their scent glands that are on their paw to additionally mark their territory.

---

19. A dog many times will curl into a ball when sleeping. This is an instinct to protect their vital organs from predators and to help them retain body heat as well.

---

20. Another method for a dog to use for cooling is panting. A panting dog has the ability to take 300 – 400 breaths without a lot of work in

comparison to his/her regular breathing at 30 – 40.

---

21. You don't often hear of the canine survivors of the Titanic. But there were three dogs who survived when the ship sank. Two were Pomeranians and One was a Pekingese. They had been in the first class cabins with their owners.

---

22. The Beatles have a song entitled "A Day in the Life". It is said that Paul McCartney recorded it with an ultrasonic whistle. This was inaudible to humans, but it is said he did it for his Shetland sheepdog.

----

23. It is cool that dogs dream much like we do as they have REM (rapid eye movement. In REM you have a tendency to remember what you are dreaming. Twitches and moving of the paws are a couple of ways to see if your pup is dreaming.

Want to know something even cooler than that? Harvard experts think that your pup is dreaming about.... Wait for it..... YOU!

---

24. Dogs are believed to be as smart as humans that are around 2 years of age and can learn about the same amount of words. Border Collies are believed to be at the top and able to comprehend up to 200 words. Poodles, Golden Retrievers, Dobermans and German Shepherds were next in line for the smartest dogs!

----

25. We assume that because a dog has a wagging tail that they are happy to see us and generally that is correct, especially if it is to the right. If the tail is over to the left it might indicate they are frightened.

If they raise their tail they could be anxious.

---

26. Dogs have a range of emotions just as humans do. They can be stressed, upset, optimistic, pessimistic. We've all seen dogs that get jealous or even depressed. But, the main emotion we enjoy seeing is that of love and affection.

---

27. Humans are not the only ones who can have stinky feet. Dogs can as well because their sweat glands are located on the pads on their paws.

---

28. It is pretty apparent that dogs and wolves are closely related. However, dogs exact lineage is a bit uncertain. We are aware that humans started training and domesticating wolves over 15,000 years ago.

----

29. Did you know that you could find your dog by their nose print just as you can find a human by their fingerprint? Each nose print is unique!

----

30. It is believed that dogs will get in alignment with the earth's magnetic field before doing their business. It is believed that they

prefer to face either north or south before doing their business. This might be TMI (too much information).

----

31. We've all seen when a dog is jealous when their owners pay attention to another dog. But scientists do not believe that dogs experience guilt. According to them those "puppy dog eyes" are probably just their reactions to being scolded.

----

32. We all know that dog urine has a powerful smell! But did you know that those acids which give it that powerful odor can also corrode metal? Maybe the lamp-post isn't the best place for them to go!

----

33. Dogs are extraordinary in their vision as they can see UV light.

They are extraordinary in the way they can sense the earth's magnetic fields, so they don't need a compass! Some believe they can even hear some of the ultrasound waves. These are the waves that bats use to navigate the dark!

----

34. The comparison between human ability to smell and dogs is simply amazing. We can just about smell a spoonful of sugar that has been put into a cup of tea. However, our dogs can smell that same spoonful of sugar in enough water to fill TWO Olympic swimming pools!

35. There has been research at Schillerhohe Hospital in Germany that has found dogs are able by smelling to determine that a human body is not working properly. This indicates that a dog could diagnose cancer. The scientist are looking forward to seeing if this is possible for diabetes or even for pre-epileptic seizures.

36. Dogs have the ability to understand up to 250 words and hand motions. Dogs can even do simple math calculations.

---

37. Looking for clever pet? Border Collies top the list with poodles, German Shepherds, Golden Retrievers and Dobermans coming in close!

---

38. You don't want your dog to be a hot dog! On a hot day when your pet is panting, take pity on them. They are wearing a large fur coat and they also have a higher body temperature than you. Humans body temperature ranges around

37 C and your canine will generally be at 38C. Fleas are attracted to their fur coat and higher body temp! Remember, dogs can only sweat through the pads of their feet!

---

39. It is believed that spaying or neutering your pet will help to prevent certain strains of cancer from developing.

---

40. You've heard of 101 Dalmatians? If left unsprayed or unneutered, a couple of dogs can produce 66,000 offspring in just six years!

----

41. The average dog can clock out at around 19 miles per hour when running full speed!

----

42. A dog has an average lifespan of 11 years. But did you know that owning a dog can cost around 14,000 dollars?

----

43. You have heard the phrase alpha dog? Generally, dogs will submit to any other dog (or human) they feel has more authority than they do.

----

44. The gestation for a female dog is approximately 60 days before her puppies are born.

----

45. Just as in humans one of the main problems for dogs is obesity.

----

46. Most people do not want to leave their pets out of the holiday festivities. It is said that 70% sign their pets name on their greeting cards.

47. The more than One hundred and fifty dog breeds have been allocated into eight various classes. Those classes include: Terrier, toy, sporting, hound, non-sporting, herding and miscellaneous.

48. Recent surveys say that the most popular dog name is Max. Coming in close are Molly, Maggie, Zach and Sam!

----

49. The sizes of dogs range from very large such as a 36 inch Great Dane who can weight 150 or more pounds, to a diminutive Chihuahua weighing in around 2 lbs.

50. Puppies should remain with their mothers until at least 8 weeks of age before being adopted.

51. Surprisingly approximately 1/3 of the dogs that are given to shelters are actually purebred.

----

52. Just because dogs have fewer taste buds (approximately 1,700 to a human's approximately 9,000); does not mean they can't be picky eaters. Since they have over 200 million scent receptors in their noses opposed to a humans 5 million it is important that the food smells and tastes good.

53. Have you heard the term "dog days"? It really has nothing to do with dogs, but has something to do with stars! In Roman times it was assumed that Sirius, the Dog Star combined with the sun's heat from July 3 – August 11. They felt this would account for the high temperatures.

54. Pete was the name of United States President Teddy Roosevelt's Pit Bull.

----

55. Barry was the most successful mountain rescue dog. He was a St. Bernard and he saved forty lives back in the 1800's.

---

56. Open a dogs mouth and you will generally find a pink tongue. Two breeds the Shar-pei as well as the Chow Chow have black tongues

57. Ever wondered who came up with the poodle's hair cut? Originally the cut was intended to improve the dog's swimming abilities. The pom-poms were not decoration, but left in place to keep their joints warm.

58. Want to know the favorite breeds of dog in the United States? That list would contain both a Labrador and Golden Retriever, Beagle, Dachshund and German Shephards.

----

59. Have you heard the term silence is golden? The only dog that does not bark in the world is the Basenji.

60. Have you ever wondered why the bus line choose the Greyhound as their name? Greyhounds are incredibly fast reaching speeds of up to 45 miles per hour!

61. Puppies can't help but be adorable even though at birth they are blind, deaf and have no teeth!

---

62. Wonder who the ever-so-great grandparent of your beloved pet is? For even the smallest of dogs the answer would be... the wolf.

---

63. Vibrissae are the whiskers found on the muzzle, above the eyes and below the jaws. These hairs are sensitive to touch and are even sensitive to air flow.

----

64. Did you ever see your dog's ears moving back and forth? They can detect the source of a sound in 6/100ths of a second. They do this

by moving their ears back and forth.

----

65. If you notice your dog's nose is often damp. This enables them to absorb various scents. They can even lick their nose to get an idea of what something "tastes" like. Have you ever noticed that when you have a stuffy nose that things just don't taste the same? It's because your sense of smell helps you to taste as well!

66. Dogs eyes can seem to glow in the dark! Their large pupils will let in more light, and they also have a "tapetum" in the rear portion of their eye. The tapetum will act almost like a mirror and reflect light to the retina. The tapetum is what makes their eyes seem to glow in the dark!

67. Want to lower your blood pressure? Get a dog! They will comfort you just with their presence. Stroking a dog is said to actually make your blood pressure go down. And dog owners are generally healthier because of increase of walking they get by owning a dog!

----

68. So who is the Empire State building in the dog world? The Great Dane

and Irish Wolfhound are the tallest dogs.

---

69. Bluey was an Australian Cattle Dog. He is the longest living dog recorded. He lived 29 years.

----

70. Because all the dogs originally came from wolves they are in fact the same species. They can breed together and produce offspring that can also breed.

----

71. The average number of breaths taken for a dog are between 10 – 30 breaths a minute.

----

72. Humans range of vision is around 180 degrees. A dog's range of vision is 250 degrees!

---

73. The French word "poupee" means doll. That is the root word of the English word "puppy".

---

74. In 17th century England many cats and dogs drowned during the flooding. Their bodies could be

viewed floating in the in the current that was racing through the street. People said it had "rained cats and dogs".

---

75. Dogs have not one, not two, but three eyelids! These eyelids help keep dirt out of their eyes.

---

76. Even in the Egyptians times dogs were wearing collars!

---

77. A dog's ears are so sensitive that rain can amplify the sound and hurt their ears.

78.. The original purpose of Dachshunds were for fighting badgers.

79.Guess how many dog's snore? Over 20%! Only 7% of cats snore!

----

80. One failed invention was the Cynophere. It was patented in 1875 by a Frenchman. It was a three-wheel vehicle that was powered by dogs on treadmills.

----

81. You have heard that dogs are "faithful"! The name Fido comes from a Latin word which means "fidelity".

82. Forty percent of all dog owners will get their dog a Christmas present!

83. You would assume that the Canary Islands were named after birds, but you would be wrong. They were named after the very large dogs living on the island.

84. Instinct is what makes your dog turn in circles before laying down. It would help flatten long grass into a bed.

---

85. A frightened dog will tuck his tail to cover his scent glands in the anal area. It will help cover his scent.

---

86. A German tax collector named Louis Dobermann, created the breed for protection while he was working.

----

87. Blue plastic boots have been issued to police dogs in Dusseldorg

German to protect their paws as they are on patrol.

---

88. Want to guess the number of dog breeds in the world? The number is over 800!

---

89. The heftiest dog recorded weighed in at 343 lbs. His name was Zorba. He was an English Mastiff. This was recorded in 1989.

90. Who hasn't heard of Rin Tin Tin? He was a German Shepherd. He was adopted from a WWI field of battle. He stared in 23 films. His contracts were signed with his paw print!

---

91. United Kingdom most popular dog names are Molly and also Max.

92.In London the dog do-do adds up to between four and five tons daily!

93.Men walking a dog are likely to have a more aggressive dog than a woman walking a dog.

----

94. The interaction of dog owners and dog amounts to a little more than two hours a day. This is actually more than the average amount of interaction with their children.

---

95. Dogs have been named the beneficiary in over one million American wills.

---

96. Laika, a Russian dog was the first canine to orbit our earth.

---

97. Instinct is what makes a dog go in circles before lying down. It helps to flatten the grass and also to get rid of insects.

---

98. Puggy has the world's longest tongue. It measured at 11.43 cm. He was a male Pekingese. This measurement was taken when he was nine years on in 2009.

---

99. In Greek mythology, Cerberus was a three-headed dog. He guarded the entrance to the underworld.

---

100. Want to have a better social life? Then get a dog. In 2000 a study indicated that walking a dog will triple your social interactions!

----

101. It is possible to teach dogs to discover by smell various cancers such as lung, breast, skin, prostate and bladder.

102.The highest selling dog went for £945.000 in 2011.

103.Bothy Twisleton-Wyke-ham-Fiennes is a Jack Russel Terrier who is the only dog that has visited both the North and South Poles.

104.The percentage of people who have had their dogs professionally photographed range around 30%.

105. A one-year old dog is at the age range of a human 16-year-old. When a dog is two years of age the equivalent is 24 human years. At the age of three it would be equivalent to 30 human years. Every subsequent year add four years.

106. The one breed that is the closest relation to a wolf is that of a pug. Which a good guess would have been a German Shepherd, so that is surprising!

---

107. The reason a dog will chase a leaving car is because they feel that they have been successful in forcing it to leave.

---

108. In the Shakespeare play "The Two Gentlemen of Verona" the only dog ever mentions was named "Crab".

---

109. When you take a walk along a Hawaiian beach called Barking Sands Beach, the sand will make a woofing and squeaking sound much like that of dog!

---

110. Pekingese puppies were carried in the sleeves of the ancient Chinese.

---

111. Pete, Teddy Roosevelt's dog, tore the pants of a visiting French Ambassador at a White House event.

---

112. Want a dog that can pee and poop when you say? Then purchase a

service dog as they also know when they are on-duty and off-duty!

----

113. In 2013 Max, who was the world's oldest dog, died at the age of 29 years and 282 days. Max was a terrier/beagle mix.

----

114. Sweetlips was George Washington's favorite fox hound.

He also had a Dalmatian coach dog he loved named Madame Moose.

115.Over half of the United States Presidents were dog owners.

116.Dog litters will average 4 – 6 puppies per litter.

117. Dogs are basically pack animals and so they do not enjoy being alone for long.

118. Want to keep your puppy warm? In ancient China they did this by putting them up their sleeves.

119. Tigger, a bloodhound, holds the world's record for longest ears. They measured at 13 inches.

---

120. The very first animal inducted in the Animal Hall of Fame was Lassie in 1969.

121. An Alaskan Malamute is able to withstand temperatures that are as low as 70 degrees before zero.

122. The stray dogs in Moscow have learned how to ride the subway in order to scavenge for food.

123. At one time it was illegal to have a pet dog in Iceland's Capital city. But in current days the laws are not as strict.

---

124. Want a dog with six toes on each foot? Then you will need to get a Norwegian Lundehund.

---

125. A pup can reach full size between the ages of twelve and twenty-four months.

----

126. Dogs can exhibit foot disorders when their toe nails get too long.

----

127. Orient who was a German Shepherd accompanied Bill Irwin,

who happened to be blind, on a hike that was 2,100 miles long on the Appalachian trail. This was accomplished in 1990 and was the first time this had happened.

---

128. Just like a human, the Chihuahuas have a soft spot in their head at birth.

---

129. The Bible mentions dogs more than 35 different times.

----

130. Want to know which breed will mature faster? The smaller breeds do so more quickly than the large breeds.

----

131. When another animal has a high pack status, then other dogs will automatically submit.

132.A state in northwestern Mexico boasts they got to name the Chihuahua as that is where they were found!

133.Dogs can walk backwards, bow, as well as salute! It just takes some patience!

134.George Washington brought his dog Sweelips into battle with him. Other soldiers did so as well.

135.Have you ever watched your dog eating grass? They do it in order to improve digestion, treating intestinal worms, fulfilling some nutritional needs or because they feel ill and most likely vomit after.

136. The smaller dogs seem to have a longer life expectance than that of larger breeds.

---

137. If you spay or neuter your dog it is believed to be preventative for certain cancers.

138. A typical dog that has a lifespan of around eleven years will cost it's owner in the range of $13,500.

---

139. A Labrador is so gently and intelligent that they make a very popular breed for dog owners. They are intelligent and obedient. They are often trained to be guide dogs.

---

140. Dogs use a variety of methods to communicate their feelings. They bark, growl, and whine. They also can use their ears and facial movements to communicate with their human friends.

---

141. The first week of a dogs life is spent sleeping (90%) and eating (10%).

---

142. Once a puppy reaches the age of one year, they are considered an adult dog.

----

143. We have all heard the term "man's best friend". It is said that this came from a lawsuit in Missouri during the 1870's. A farmer sued his neighbor for shooting his dog.

----

144. When a dog smiles (shows his teeth), that is not a sign of friendship, but is a sign of aggression.

---

145. Dogs are much better able to see moving objects than those that are still. If you are trying to get your dogs attention try waving your arms and moving around.

---

146. The term "toy dogs" or "lap dogs" came to be because the pets are so little they look like toys and because of their diminutive size they can fit on your lap!

---

147. Raisins, Grapes, Chocolate, Onion, and Garlic are all things you should not feed your dog. It can make them sick.

---

148. Want to know the first thing to teach your dog? Sit!

---

149. When a puppy takes something away, don't chase him. Instead run away from your puppy and he will think you are playing and come after you.

---

150. Humans cannot see nearly as well in the dark as our canine friends. They have a special light reflecting layer hidden behind their eyes!

----

151. The heaviest dog weighed in at 343 pounds. He was eight feet and three inches long. This was in 1989. He was an Old English Mastiff.

----

152. Ozzy Osborn's wife's dog was taken by a coyote. Ozzy wrestled until the coyote let go of his wife's dog.

----

153. Kubla Khan owned the most dogs on record. He had 5,000 Mastiffs! That's a lot of Kibble!

----

154. Paulding, Ohio gets to boast having the weirdest law. A police

officer is allowed to bite the dog to get it to be quiet!

---

155. Without proving that your dog is either a hunting dog or a guard dog, it is against the law to own one.

---

156. Spain has cave paintings of dogs over 12,000 years in age!

----

157. Which dog has the best nose? The Bloodhound! They have been tracking down criminals since the Middle Ages.

----

158. Which dogs love to hear themselves talk? The Beagle and Border Collie are both big barkers!

159. Did you know that 33% of people will leave messages for their dogs on answering machines or talk to their dogs on the phone when away?

----

160. France comes in second in dog population, but the United States will get First Place!

161. Have you ever met a 15-year-old? Well your one year old dog is just a mature as a 15 year old!

----

162. When watching TV, 87% of dog owners claim that their dogs will curl up either beside them or at their feet.

----

163. Want to know the canine family list? Dogs, coyotes, jackals, foxes and wolves!

---

164. Ever wondered how come your dog knows exactly when it is time to eat, or when an owner should be home? Dogs are gifted with an internal clock.

---

165. Without exercise a dog has no way to release the pent up energy that it has been storing all day!

----

166. Want a dog that can be between one and twenty-nine different colors? Well then a Chihuahua is the one for you!

----

167. Puppies are born with no teeth. Little puppy teeth are extremely sharp! But, they will lose those baby teeth and get permanent teeth around six weeks and two month of age.

----

168. The birth-mother of a dog will keep the puppy warm, fed and clean. The puppy should be with his mother at a minimum of seven

weeks. Around eight weeks old the puppy is able to live on his/her own without mom.

169.An average puppy will sleep for about 14 hours daily, but that can easily go up to 19 hours. They take naps and sleep at night.

---

170. Puppies are required by law to have certain vaccinations after birth.

---

171. It will take over a year of training for a guide dog to be ready to be placed with a family.

---

172. Before getting a family or companion a service or guide dog must pass a test!

173.A guide dog is taught to focus only on the one person he/she is assisting and to ignore everyone else. They are taught to ignore food and attention.

174.Guide dogs are not cheap. They cost around $20,000

175. Don't pet or talk to a guide/service dog without first checking with his/her owner.

176. Labradors make wonderful guide/service dogs.

177.It takes eight to ten years before an adult guide dog will retire.

178.Guide dogs can go into restaurants, clinics, hospital, stores, hotels, movie theaters, beaches, and many other places. They can also travel on a variety of transportations!

----

179. Guide dogs are trained to walk in a straight line in the center of the pavement and to guide around any obstacles.

----

180. Guide dogs only turn corners when told to.

----

181. Greeks, Persians, Babylonians and Assyrians were some of the first known to use dogs to help with law enforcement.

---

182. European Police Department used bloodhounds over 200 years ago to catch criminals.

---

183. Police Teams Used dogs during WWI and also during WWII

----

184. German Shepherd are the most common dog to be used in Police work. They are smart and aggressive.

----

185. Some criminals can be deterred by just a low growl and just the presence of the police dog.

186. Police dogs make their home with their companion officer.

---

187. Police dogs can sniff out substances that might be illegal or dangerous!

188. The police dog is not only taught to locate bombs or explosives, they are also trained to be very careful and to show their partner exactly where the danger is located.

----

189. A dog can hear four times better than a person.

----

190. Dogs drink by having their tongues slap the water and pull in into their mouth where the close their mouth over it to swallow.

----

191. Although it is not recommended to do this, 45% of dogs sleep in bed with their human friends.

----

192. About 30% of Dalmatians are deaf in at least one ear. This is usually a genetic issue.

---

193. Nitrogen in dog urine will cause lawn burns. Yards that have been fertilized seem to burn more easily.

---

194. Dog urine has information that other dogs will be able to tell their

sex, age and even what mood they are in.

---

195. Dogs are amazing in the fact that they can detect medical issues. Some dogs can sense when a person will have a epileptic seizure.

---

196. You don't need a lie detector test with a dog. They instinctively

know when we are lying. They know if you are trustworthy or not.

---

197. Baboons have been seen keeping dogs for pet and protection.

---

198. During Vietnam over 4,500 dogs were sent in to help the troops in battle.

199.If you have seen a dog eat poop then most probably you thought that is disgusting. But there are several reasons behind this behavior such as Hunger or Food Obsession. Also several diseases or illnesses can make a dog to eat feces. Lastly if the dog is under anxiety and fear may eat his/her stool.

200. A dog's bite has 320 pounds of pressure compared to a human measured to be 120 pounds. The tests were performed on an American pit bull terrier and a Rottweiler.

CONCLUSION

Dogs are your loyal loving companions. When you own one then you know how and where to pet your dog or what food he/she love best or even what games they enjoy most.

But even though you know so much about your canine friend, there are a few…… or a lot of DOG FACTS you might didn't know and which you probably have read in this book.

If you found this book useful please consider leaving an honest review.

                          Thank you!

Made in United States
Troutdale, OR
12/21/2023